The
MOONLIGHT DREAMS

By

Meg AkuSika De Amasi

"LIFE DEVOID OF DREAMS IS EMPTY"
- Delve Into

"WORDS ARE LIKE PRECIOUS PEARLS
WORN TO ANNOUNCE A PRESENCE"
- Meg De Amasi

"BEAUTIFUL THOUGHTS MAKE
BEAUTIFUL WORDS"
- Dr Wayne W. Dyer

Publications by Meg AkuSika De Amasi:

Butterflies, Tears and Flowers

The Roots and Fruits of the Matter

The Talking Drums -Eco from Slavery to Freedom

Verses, Senses and Beyond

ACKNOWLEDGEMENT

Grateful to Anne Clark for the foreword and editing

Esther Cobblah Akotia for type setting and publishing

COPYRIGHT

DEDICATION

This book of poems is dedicated to my Higher Self

My teacher, my All - in-All

Every moment is beautiful

Every thought is beautiful

Every word is inspiring

Keep smiling, keep hoping

Keep loving, Life is beautiful

Meg AkuSika De Amasi

CONTENTS

Foreword

Meg Amasi's little book of poems is full of the warmth and joyousness of the Africa she evokes, which offers 'a blessed welcome at every door', but it is also haunted by a sense of loss of the motherland. It is not an accident that the collection opens with a poem about separation - the separation of birth - and the clear-eyed perception that 'freedom stings' underpins the gentle optimism which is the keynote of the book. If you want to understand the experience of exile and adaptation, read her companion poems *First Impressions* and *My New Home*, which were published in Scottish PEN's on-line magazine *New Writing*, where the editors commented on their authenticity of voice. If you want to understand her passionate attachment to Africa, read the evocative *Nostalgia* and *My Roots Too Deep.*

The poems acknowledge the difficulties, even – in poems like *Mothers' Watch and Her Heart Yields to Life* – the cruelties of life but they are essentially affirmative: 'failure is not my name' asserts the final poem, while poems such as *Wisdom and Old Age* and *Princess Scota of Egypt* testify to the enriching strength of a desire to 'explore greater fields' and not be content with living 'one life for a century'. Above all, Meg sees the world as a place of transit, in which we are 'all refugees', all bound on an adventure, all solaced by 'moonlight dreams' and by the enduring power of love and, of course, poetry.

A C Clarke

SWEET MOTHER

FREEDOM WITH STRINGS

In my mother's womb I kicked and punched;
a cry for freedom, a yearning for adventure
in a New World. Nine months? I popped out at seven.
Freedom! I'm out I tried to say, but choked
on slimy green mucus.
A sharp slap on the buttocks, permanent
finger marks for posterity.
Truth awakened: aah, freedom stings!
Freedom comes with strings attached.

SANDS OF TIME

In Psalm 139; "You are fearfully and wonderfully
made"
Let it be your guide in life.
It was only yesterday, a tiny bundle of joy arrived,
a precious gift, a Taurus and as bold.
She loves, she cares.
Each life she enters - ripples of kindness flow.
As the sands of time trickle, she wonders
what's coming her way. She's told; "You're born to be
great"Be open to receive and achieve.

MOTHERS' WATCH

Stream flooded again, mothers can't cross
Seat of patience, watching over hunger stricken
infants.
On the other bank, heartless folks feed on fattened
cows
crumbs thrown to the rapids.
Mothers watch like hungry wolfs smelling a prey,
but can't get to it.
Pray for the rains to cease,
flood to abate,
mothers will cross the stream.
Infants will feed.

HER HEART YIELDS TO LIFE

There she lay raped of her treasures,
trampled upon by strangers.
Her hair caked in red mud, shredded sack cloth
exposed her womanhood, the shame, the shame.

Suckling babes snatched from her malnourished
breasts
on baked earth, sprawled and left for dead.
Clenched fists held a secret.
The men returned not to rescue,
but to make a claim.
She held on steadfast daring them
heartless, they cut her hands off.

Pain and anger rise to her throat.
She stands no chance, but she's not for giving in
for her children's sake, her heart yields to life.

(This poem is in honour of Sierra Leonean women
victims of war)

FATHER'S LOVE AT A GLANCE

A PERFECT FATHER

Strong protective arms, as bold as a lion
Keeps vigil and guardsjealously over, even, the unruly.
He's earned himself a few unsavoury names:
hard - hearted, unyielding...disciplinarian...,
but look inside his heart - tender and caring -
all he aspires, success for his brood.

LOOKING UP TO A FATHER

I look up to you from the moment our eyes met
You love me, gave me a name so precious.
Expected me to walk in your steps to grow as big.
I tried.
On your broad shoulders, I gained a grandstand view
of the world.
Permanent reminder of father's unwavering love.

FOND MEMORIES OF A FATHER

I thirst for years gone by.
We use to sit at the little table under the deeming
hurricane light.
Most magical moments learning your favourite songs.
Oh, the invented silly stories - hours of fun
I learnt to laugh without a care; you will be around forever.

You taught me to count, I'm still counting the days
we shall meet again.

"A father's love is like a misty rain coming softly, but
flooding the river"
African proverb

ROMANCE ON THE MIND

LOVE GIVES THE HEART A HOOK.

When the moon dismiss the night clouds,
when the sun burns a white hole
in the center of clear blue sky,
a heart full of love does not see offence.
The heart looks up, love gives it a hook.

LOVE IN CONTROL

Love, not overly concerned to please
the whims of the heart; to love and to cherish.
To love and be loved.
Love desires, only, to release a chemistry
that stops the heart faltering.

A WHISPERING SPIRIT

In the heart, emotions arise and flow,
induced by a whisper from the spirit
soft, gentle - can be missed.
So fleeting - easily taken for granted.
Like the dove, it knows where and when to land;
bearing love - whispering peace.

FORGETTING ME NOT

You may sweep me under the carpet- forgotten.
I'll forget you not.
Seed of love already sown
deep down in the atrium of the heart
there, it remains buried for eternity,
forgetting you not.

MOONLIGHT DREAMS

Moonlight dreams come only
when the silvery sky glitters - no sun.
The night birds sweetly sing love songs
that melt the heart and sends the earth into a stupor
dreaming dreams of hope under the light of
tranquillity.
Shhh... tread gently, lest the peace is broken
Earth, woken too soon, disturbs the moonlight
dreams.

I'M PURE GOLD

I'm pure gold
don't touch me
I might melt with the kiss of your heat
I'm a metal, don't love me
I might choke the life out of you
Keep me safe, adore me, I'm a treasure – a glittering
gold.

LIFE'S ROLLER COASTER

THE BRAVE ONE

I've known you to be brave
not the weakling you portray.
A strike of your bare hand, many giants dead at your
feet.
Many good deeds to your credit.
Hands are now chaffed, old and tired.
Sparkles in the eyes dimming.
Smile faintly, lips quiver.
Distance look in the eyes, betray of desires unfulfilled
only consolation, strength in your laughter of old.
Take heart, no one ever achieved all in a life time.

WISP OF SMOKE

How could you've got it so wrong? She asked wearily
disappointment plastered her face
She knew me well, she felt my pain.
Yes, life can be a wisp of smoke
like the grass, cold wind quickly freezes it
hot air quickly kills it.
Barren land holds no strength and
sustains no life until the smoke is lifted.

IN THE FAST LANE

Many windows of opportunities open
none received my attention.
So also have I indulged myself in many fields,
none received my passion.
Arriving from the rapids, common sense demands
a break- just as easy, shutting out wasted years
closing all fake windows. Calm after the storm, vision
expands be yonder.

WISDOM AND OLD AGE

Wisdom and old age - a mismatch.
wisdom isn't always ripe with age
it strides in with grey hair, winkles, knock knees,
increasing painand memory loss.
Grey hair does not come with wisdom neither does
time.
Live one life for a century, wisdom will not thread your
borders.
Live a century with one life; cup overflows with
wisdom.
All down to choices you've made while running for the
century.

GLAD YOU'RE STILL HERE WITH US

Bitten the odds - proverbial three score years.
Congratulations. Only one hindrance - can't skip
in the playground any more. Dear me, need a hand
to prop you up, to spoon feed you and spring clean
your home.
Dignity may have abandoned you,
we the kindred spirits have not.
Glad you're still here cheering us up with your old
antics.

SEEDS OF GREATNESS

Every ground we trod,
in the sprint and print of every footstep
seeds of love impressed, cautiously nurturing,
boldly transforming-seeds of greatness in the making.

THE WHISPERING SPIRIT

In the heart, where feelings and emotions arise and
flowinduced by a gentle whisper from the spirit.
Soft, gentle – can be missed.
So fleeting- easily taken for granted.
Like the dove, it knows where and when to land,
bearing love, whispering peace.

REWARDS

The seed you planted, not died in vain
love you gave, not withered with time
faith you held – steadfast
Time prevails-rewards multi - fold.

CONTEMPLATING – WHAT IS IT?

FOREST'S SHADOW

Full glow of love deep in the forest's shadow
soaked walking in heavy dew, I watch as the heat
of morning sun forcefully parts the thicket,
rays of sunshine reach my weary face,
spirit revived for that moment, up and up I ventured
reached the mountain top gasping.
Long I stand, long I look
magical world I see.
At the East, a radiant cross beams love
on my restless spirit,
partaking in its glory, I heaved a sigh of gratitude.

I FOUND HEAVEN ON EARTH

By the waters,
I dreamt of heavenly beams of
stars and night skies. Forth come Angels of love,
forth stretch hands of welcome
forth went I in an embrace.
By the waters, sat I contented,
having found heaven on earth.

YOU MADE ME TO LAST

I'm, but dust from the earth, you made me.
One breath, life instilled.
Water of life flow freely in my veins
continually refreshing and renewing
Out of the mouth came living words and spoken
wisdomupon which I set my identity.
In hope I live and thrive. By faith, I'm enabled
to share the testimony of profound love.
My maker downloaded sound mind into my head.
Love into my heart and good health into my being.
I'm a child of God – made to last.

IN THE SENSORY GARDEN

It was just me - oblivious.
Occasional breeze didn't stir
plants unperturbed, so was I.
Sitting reading, something made me look up
I saw a stone shaped like a mushroom,
something perched on it and thought
it was a stone too. Then the bird dipped its head to
drink.
I willed it to stay so I could take a picture.
It read my mind and flew away.

MEGGY JUST ARRIVED IN SCOTLAND!

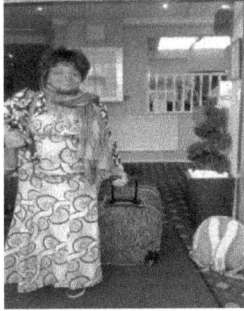

FIRST IMPRESSIONS

My nervous sleep was interrupted.
"Dundas Bus Station" said the husky voice,
the rest, mumble and jumble.
"Please, what did he say?" I asked the lady who had
shared my journey
"I canny hear you" she replied. Her raw tone threw
me back.
With African politeness, I said; "Thank you Madam"
I collected my belongings, left her where I'd found her.
"Thank you too!" hit the back of my head.
I didn't turn to see her frown.

Cont'd on next page

First Impressions cont'd

The concourse was full of people waiting expectantly
"Dundas Bus Station" the one thing that felt familiar.
Sister Smith had promised; "I'll meet you there
Nurse... "
I waited for hours shivering from the spring chill
clutching
her letter of invitation, the only thing that said
"I belong"
My afro hair stood sharp against the straight locks of
Glaswegian lassies.
My dark skin yearned for Shea butter cream and heat
of yesterday's sun.
I heard two men: "This wee lassie's waiting fae
someone ..."

One approached me: great to be noticed!
"You all right? Want a taxi?"
"Yes please, I'm going to Royal Maternity Hospital
please"
Still polite, too naive to know I would change.
I lent him my precious invitation letter and his face
said:
"You will be OK".

MY NEW HOME

The taxi drove me around, over and about
George Square and City Chambers passing a few
too many times.
Just as I was soaking in the beautiful city,
we arrived at some blocks of dim old buildings
right on top of a steepest hill. Surely, not a maternity
hospital-more like a mortuary!
"This is Rottenrow, Hen" Taxi driver announced- a job
well done.
The name baffled me, but I said nothing. I paid the
fare and watched him drive away leaving me in the
grim cold place.

Cont'd on next page

My New Home cont'd

I never saw Sister Smith, but I found warmth and
comfortinside the 'Nurses Home.
My second life began here taking a different turn
in a land where kindness mingled with cold wind, grey
skies and rain.
I learnt the lessons of how not to be.

I discovered one day that Dundas Bus Station was only
a minute away,
not what the taxi driver made it to be, but still, I'm
grateful for his deceit.
It helped me fall in love; brown eyes peering from a
Black Cab
fright in them softening, as each street showed
there was nothing to fear. But, on that particular day,
I needed more than a minute; a big bowl of pounded
yams and pepper soup.
These, I had traded in for mince and tatties!

NOSTALGIA

THE TALKING DRUMS

At dawn, as I lie contemplating far from my ancestral
home
a heavy duvet takes over from soft linen garments
drapes and protects me from the cold breeze. In a
trance,
I fall in tune with the Talking Drums.
Family chants,
the five o'clock cock-crow add to my sense of loss.
I hear the deep vibrations synchronising with my
heart beats;
each rhythm, a chant of ballads past. Each beat, a
note adding
to the songs of my life.(Cont'd)

The Talking Drums cont'd
"Wake up my children, rise up and see what I yearn to
feel again each day.
Look to the East and fix your eyes on my favourite
mountain,
to the West and walk the roads that I know so well.
A feeling of nostalgia takes my joy away. My cries faint
in my real world - under the cloak of Western warmth.

I'm African - I am me!
Where're the Comforters? I asked.
They will come. They will come.
I put aside my dreams for tomorrow morning
and now I shall make the best of today.
African woman in Diaspora,
I know where my heart belongs.

MY KIND OF AFRICA

My kind of Africa, great ancestral mythology
True love and genuine hospitality,
a blessed welcome at every door -
once experienced, forever smitten.
Africa, a magnet for the rich and poor.
My kind of Africa, banana leaves will dance a freedom
dance
no more confusing drum notes, diversity with no
adversity,
one Africa, one entity.
A benevolent dictator would purify blood diamonds
create a wealth of nations to be proud of
"Backward never- Forward ever"

MY ROOTS TOO DEEP

A look over the great ocean,
mountains, valleys and deserts,
a separation from my Mother's apron strings.
Tempted to feel melancholy. No need.
Tides of separation, an illusion.
My roots too deep,
my dreams for Africa far too big to ever die.

IN DIVERSITY WE LIVE

Human race is always on the move- can't be stopped.
We've journeyed all over the world
arriving in Scotland wearing different colour skins:
brown, black, yellow, pink and white.
Some came with straight hair, some curly hair and
dreadlocks.

It's challenging with the blonds and brunettes.
Dark, black and red hair, much more so with
brown, blue, green and grey eyes.
Add exotic lips, exotic eyes and exotic dialects-jigsaw
complete.

No kidding, some arrived wearing Sarees, Kaftans, the
Burka and Karba.
SalwarKameez, turbans and the Kilt - Steeped in
different cultures.
No turning back, keep talking, keep mixing,
keep loving.
What you call home or country no longer relevant,
we're all émigré walking the walk.

BY MY ANCESTRAL LOOK

My own palace by Stirling Castle,
but by my ancestral looks, I may have 'failed'
my citizenship test. Certainly not,
failure is not my name.
All I know for sure; no one will ever be me.
In my own African ways, history is made.
My 'Africanisms' - inscribed on a tablet-
'Stone of Destiny'
I claim the best of both worlds.

PRINCESS SCOTA OF EGYPT

Strong ancestry,
desire to explore greater fields.
In turbulent seas she sailed into the
land of red haired and kilted men.
Brave Hearts, warriors to be reckoned with.
By her queenly charms, they submitted to her rule
In return, she gave their country her name.
Scotland, a lasting legacy.

WHEN THE SPIRIT CALLS

If I was told, I would have dismissed the idea.
Never was it my intention to abandon the land of
Africa.
Nor was it my desire to seek new horizons.
Spirit of the forest kept me happy.
Simple life, yet contended surrounded and protected.
I roamed freely; miles and miles all alone – no fear.
I talked to the wild flowers, watched the bees
burrowing deep for tiny drops of nectar. I stopped to
admire the ants busy on their line of duty. Birds flew,
danced and dived in the sky – they even had their
own language. Always amazed as how tiny creatures
could surmount such ginormous feat. I'll do
something big one day I promised.

Then Lorries started climbing the big mountains,
albeit, with much difficulties to reach my village. I
travelled to big towns. I travelled on big boats on big
rivers. I wasn't happy any more- I missed the spirit of
the forest. It wasn't long when a call came – the
mighty spirit of the world called upon my sacrifice. I
sojourned in the Free Land for a year, forty years on,
like the Children of Israel, I'm still in the wilderness.
Suffice to say it hasn't been in vain- I've managed to
build my own ant hill in Scotland - that's progress.

QUOTES

"There comes a time when you need to stop talking, release the matter, gather your confidence, go forward, and make things happen" Bill Wayne

"You cannot give what you do not have- attain your height first, you will have plenty to give when you have it all then no one can pull you down"Meg Amasi

"Every day in every way, I'm getting better and better. Yes, I am. Yes, I am" Emile Coue

"Once, I was totally immobile with fear. I did all the hard work no one wanted to do. I couldn't speak. I called upon the great speakers to speak for me. No one knew what I did behind closed doors. I gave others the honour they didn't deserve" Meg De Amasi

"Your greatest fear may lead you to your greatest achievement – if you can't speak it, write it even when you feel fear" Meg De Amasi

Reference Wikipedia

A ship said to have sailed from Egypt with Scota and family.(Scota (left) with GoídelGlas voyaging from Egypt, as depicted in a 15th century manuscript of the Scotichronicon of Walter Bower; in this version Scota and GoídelGlas (Latinized as Gaythelos) are wife and husband. Although these legends vary, they all agree that Scota was the eponymous founder of the Scots and that she also gave her name to Scotland. (Source-Wikipedia)

THE MOONLIGHT DREAMS BY MEG AKU SIKA DE AMASI

ABOUT THE POEM

Meg De Amasi's little book of poems is full of the warmth and joyousness of the Africa she evokes, which offers 'a blessed welcome at every door', but it is also haunted by a sense of loss of the motherland. It is not an accident that the collection opens with a poem about separation - the separation of birth - and the clear-eyed perception that 'freedom stings' underpins the gentle optimism which is the keynote of the book. A.C Clarke

ABOUT THE AUTHOR

"Even without drumbeats, banana leaves dance"

Meg AkuSika De Amasi is an African Poet and author based in Stirling Scotland. She continues to dance and thrive, writing poems that resonate with her African and Scottish heritage she shares in her latest book, The Moonlight Dreams. Keen on women and equality issues, she founded the African Caribbean Women Association- ACWA. She was also one of the main movers and first Chair of Meridian – First Black and Ethnic Minority Women Project in Glasgow. She is an award winning community activist and campaigner. Awarded "Take Action Award" 2013, by Sheila McKecnie Foundation (SMK) sponsored by Age UK on Sickle Cell Disease Campaign in Scotland. In 2014, she received Stirling Council Provost's Civic Award for her outstanding contributions to the communities in Stirling. Meg qualifies herself as a Lifter, Enabler and a Giver, empowering, particularly, women and children to maximise their life chances. She sees herself as a social engineer and entrepreneur. A Motivational Speaker and a Licensed Workshop Leader for "Heal Your Life" by Louise M Hay.

Love Life, Be Healed.

Best wishes - Meg

Copyright -ISBN 0-9546323-4-6   2015

www.ingramcontent.com/pod-product-compliance
Lightning Source LLC
Chambersburg PA
CBHW060950050426
42337CB00052B/3407